Redeeming Your
TIMELINE

STUDY GUIDE

Redeeming Your TIMELINE

SUPERNATURAL SKILLSETS FOR HEALING PAST WOUNDS, CALMING FUTURE ANXIETIES, AND DISCOVERING REST IN THE NOW

TROY A. BREWER

DESTINY IMAGE® PUBLISHERS, INC.
P.O. Box 310, Shippensburg, PA 17257-0310
"Promoting Inspired Lives."

This book and all other Destiny Image and Destiny Image Fiction books are available at Christian bookstores and distributors worldwide.

Cover design by Eileen Rockwell
Interior design by Terry Clifton

For more information on foreign distributors, call 717-532-3040.
Reach us on the Internet: www.destinyimage.com.

ISBN 13 TP: 978-0-7684-5955-5

For Worldwide Distribution, Printed in the U.S.A.
1 2 3 4 5 6 7 8 / 25 24 23 22 21

Contents

Welcome to Redeeming Your Timeline!

Hi! I'm Troy Brewer, the author of *Redeeming Your Timeline*, the book you are about to study. Let me warn you from the start—you'll need your Bible open during this study! The Bible is about time from beginning to end. But it also has a timeless perspective because it's God's Word, and God speaks outside time. But we're getting ahead of ourselves.

As you will discover in the Introduction of the book, time is a big deal. We are also going to discover that redemption is a big deal. If there is no redemption, then time is nothing but a slow death to all creation. If you make a big deal out of time, you have to make a big deal out of redemption—and we are going to do that in a really big way.

I hope you noticed the subtitle to this book and study: *Supernatural Skillsets for Healing Past Wounds, Calming Future Anxieties*, and *Discovering Rest in the Now*. It highlights what I mean by "timeline"—your past, future, and present. You can only live in the now, but your past and what you think or fear about the future definitely affects how you live right now. If God's Word is a lamp unto my feet and a light unto my path, then it sheds light on where I've been (past), where I'm going (future), and where I am. Not only that, but because God operates outside of time, He has access to your past and future as surely as He is present in your now. He sovereignly reigns magnificently over all of time. And when you learn what this can mean, it makes a huge difference in how you see your past, present, and future. Hope rises; change is possible; miracles happen.

You're already well on the way in your timeline. You don't know when it will come to an end, but you know Someone who does. Are you ready to have His help in redeeming that timeline? Whatever age you are right now, I can tell you that time is short. Today is the day of salvation! Don't miss all that God has to tell you in the next few days—He will make an eternity of difference in your life.

Let's get going! As He promised, Jesus is with us to the end of the age!

Troy Brewer

Leader and User Guides (Read This First)

- This workbook will serve a dual purpose: as a guide for individuals who are eager to discover what God's Word tells us about time and to offer suggestions for small group leaders and participants with questions and content that will help them apply the Scriptures and content of the book *Redeeming Your Timeline*.

- The sessions will be based on multiple chapters. Whether you are studying alone or in a small group, as you read the assigned chapters, take a moment to jot down your thoughts after the reflection questions as the end of each chapter. These will help you as you work on the lesson on your own or with others.

[NOTE: Leader notes will be enclosed in brackets and shaded.]

[Make sure to secure a copy of the book *Redeeming Your Timeline* as well as a copy of this workbook for each group member.

KEY: Encourage everyone to read the first book assignment (Introduction and Chapters One through Five) before the first session. You may even want to have a preliminary session to pass out the materials and let the group meet one another.]

- This workbook has three parts: Front Matter (what you're reading now); Study Sessions (the five discussion guides); and Leader/Group Helps (tools to make this and further small group studies great for you).

- Each session will include enough material to gather for between an hour and two, plus a daily follow-up alongside the reading of the next chapter in *Redeeming Your Timeline*. Decide as a group how long you want the sessions to be and handle the content that way.

- Note throughout this workbook that I've written the quoted Scripture verses in **bold** so that we are all clear when God is speaking to us.

- As noted in the Welcome, the ideal approach for participants would be to read the entire *Redeeming Your Timeline* book straight through and then re-read each chapter assignment during the week it will be the focus of the session. At a minimum, group members should read the assigned chapters of the week. Participation and learning will be severely hampered if you are not prepared.

[Be sure to check out the Leader/Group Helps section for lots of resources and suggestions from others who have been down the same road.]

Outline for Each Session

The following notes give you a sense of the flow and components of each of the sessions.

[Leaders should note the approximate time allotted for each part of the session, so you can keep on track with the agreed length of the sessions.]

Title

The session titles reflect the chapter sections in the book, highlighting the five premises that underlie this teaching:

1. God created time. He is not subject to or shackled by it in any way.

2. God created time for the purpose of works of redemption.

3. Redemption changes everything.

4. You can introduce redemption into any part of your timeline (past, present, future) and it changes everything within your timeline, including space and matter.

5. We are stewards—not owners—of our lives. As priests, we apply the blood. As kings, we bring Kingdom dominion into all that we steward, including time.

Memory Verse

A Bible verse will be suggested for memorization/meditation in each session. It will relate to the main theme of the study for that week.

[Encourage members of the group to memorize and offer opportunities for them to recite individually or as a group. Point out times when the memory verse comes up in discussion.]

Redeeming Your Timeline Reading Assignment for This Week

Unlike many books, *Redeeming Your Timeline* includes reflection questions and comments at the close of each chapter. These should be used as part of preparation for the group sessions or to supplement your individual study.

Preparing

A brief opening thought will set the stage for the themes and content of the session. It may include highlights from the assigned reading in *Redeeming Your Timeline*.

This section will include some warm-up questions to help the group focus on the theme for the session and perhaps review a previous discussion.

[Use some or all of these questions depending on the level of interaction by the group. Also included will be some group activities and "housekeeping" suggestions involving hosting duties, prayer requests, group contact information, etc.]

Timeless Words

This section will introduce one or more key Bible passages related to the theme and explore the group's understanding of the content in the book reading assignment.

Here you will find some space for your own notes and perhaps some clarifying notes that may help in the discussion.

[The questions will review the reading assignment, focus on clarifying the biblical passages, and emphasize observation: What do these readings say? Those who complete the questions included at the end of the chapter will be more prepared to interact during the group sessions.]

Study Notes

When needed or helpful, this section will offer some additional insights from the Scripture passages being used, which may be helpful during the discussion or for further study.

[Review these in preparing to lead the discussion. The notes may answer some questions that come up in the group.]

Discerning the Times

Several questions will now focus on the wider significance and principles related to the content of the biblical and book readings. What do these readings *mean*?

[Here the objective is for the group to work toward a clear grasp of the biblical truth or truths found in the study readings and how these truths relate to daily living.]

Timely Words

The underlying point of gathering and studying God's Word together is the practical question of personal action. When we learn, the lesson will soon fade and be forgotten if we don't apply it to our lives. Here we will discuss specific actions we may undertake as a result of what we've discussed in the session.

[Here the purpose will be to help group members engage personally with the challenges found in the book. How does understanding God's Word and His call to me *affect my life*?]

Final Matters

This section will include reminders to share prayer requests.

It will also offer a closing thought from Pastor Troy as the group ends the session.

Redeeming Your Timeline Reading Assignment for Next Week

Daily Follow-Up

Here you will find five follow-up Scripture readings with a brief devotional question to encourage journaling and prayer between sessions.

[Encourage your group members to use these and consider including the daily questions in your discussions during the sessions.]

Session One

What Is Time?

Memory Verse

My times are in Your hand; deliver me from the hand
of my enemies, and from those who persecute me.
—Psalm 31:15

From the moment we are conceived until the moment we leave this earth, the clock is ticking. We are creatures of time, but we were designed for eternity. The same David who was inspired by the Holy Spirit to write this week's memory verse also wrote Psalm 139:16: ***Your eyes saw my substance, being yet unformed. And in Your book they all were written, the days fashioned for me, when as yet there were none of them.*** He understood that every moment of his life was not only known by God, but controlled by God's hand. All of this makes it crucial that we understand time and how God uses it as He shapes us for and guides us to eternity.

Redeeming Your Timeline Reading Assignment for This Session

Introduction and Chapters One through Five (pages 7–62)

Preparing

Questions to help you engage with the themes for the session. [If the group is new and doesn't know one another, make sure you have name tags or take time to have each person introduce themselves briefly.]

[The questions will always be written as if you are asking them. Consider assigning a member each time to ask the questions. Feel free to use only some of the questions or alter the wording to fit your style or the group's. Encourage the group members to bring both their Bibles and their copy of *Redeeming Your Timeline* to each session.]

1.   Read the five premises on Page 10. Pastor Troy's conclusion is that Jesus is a time traveler who is just as willing to work in your past as He is in your present and future. (Page 11) Do you agree? What questions or concerns does this bring to your mind?

_____

_____

_____

_____

_____

2.   Pastor Troy borrowed a definition from Einstein to help us start thinking about time (temporary) in the light of eternity (permanent): "Time is God's way of keeping everything from happening at once." What is God's purpose for time and why does Pastor Troy call time "a gift from God"? (Pages 18-19)

_____

_____

_____

_____

_____

3.   Considering Genesis 1:1, what has God revealed to you about the time/space continuum? (Pages 23-24) How does that continuum also apply to past, present, future, redeemed and unredeemed time? (Pages 33-38) How does it apply to matter or to space?

_____

_____

_____

_____

Timeless Words

The following Bible passages are central to the opening chapters of *Redeeming Your Timeline*. Let's hear them read as we follow along, and we will include these verses in our conversation about the book.

[Ask two different people to read the passages below out loud. Choose from the questions and notes to shape your discussion, but encourage people to give personal feedback from their reading.]

Psalm 139:1-5 (TPT):

[1] *You perceive every movement of my heart and soul, and you understand my every thought before it even enters my mind.*

[2] *You are so intimately aware of me, Lord.*

[3] *You read my heart like an open book and you know all the words I'm about to speak before I even start a sentence!*

[5] *You know every step I will take before my journey even begins.*

[6] *You've gone into my future to prepare the way, and in kindness you follow behind me to spare me from the harm of my past.*

Ecclesiastes 3:1-11:

[1] *To everything there is a season, a time for every purpose under heaven:*

[2] *A time to be born, and a time to die; a time to plant, and a time to pluck what is planted;*

[3] *A time to kill, and a time to heal; a time to break down, and a time to build up;*

[4] *A time to weep, and a time to laugh; a time to mourn, and a time to dance;*

⁵ A time to cast away stones, and a time to gather stones; a time to embrace, and a time to refrain from embracing;

⁶ A time to gain, and a time to lose; a time to keep, and a time to throw away;

⁷ A time to tear, and a time to sew; a time to keep silence, and a time to speak;

⁸ A time to love, and a time to hate; a time of war, and a time of peace.

⁹ What profit has the worker from that in which he labors?

¹⁰ I have seen the God-given task with which the sons of men are to be occupied.

¹¹ He has made everything beautiful in its time. Also He has put eternity in their hearts, except that no one can find out the work that God does from beginning to end.

4. What was the special anointing of the tribe of Issachar? Why would that be a powerful gift? (Page 45) How does that correspond to Deuteronomy 28:66-67 and the curse of being out of timing? (Page 48)

_____

_____

_____

_____

5.   What is the difference between times and seasons? How do you these two kinds of time work in your life? (Pages 49-53)

6.   What are the main points about time that Solomon was making in Ecclesiastes 3:1-11?

7.   On pages 34–40, Pastor Troy defines and contrasts *unredeemed time* and *redeemed time*. How are these major time categories different from each other?

8. Read Psalm 139:1-5 in the The Passion Translation. How did the psalmist (likely David) understand God is not subject to time, space or matter? Why would Jesus want to spare you from the harm of your past? How do you think that would "prepare a way" in your future? (Page 60)

Study Notes

The Bible doesn't spend a lot of time trying to prove there is a God—it simply takes God as the ultimate starting point. Exactly what we would expect God to do. The universe is proof that God exists because it is not self-existent. It came from somewhere—or from Someone.

Notice how modern science tries to use time to disprove or discount God. As if adding a few billion years here and there will make a difference in the process of nothing becoming something and then something becoming, accidentally and without purpose, everything. God's Word shows us both sides of the conflict: ***"The heavens declare the glory of God, and the firmament shows His handiwork"*** (Psalm 19:1) and ***"The fool has said in his heart, 'There is no God'"*** (Psalm 14:1). Given the choice, God's witness is more truthful than man's.

Ecclesiastes 3:1-11 reminds us that there is *"a time"* not "time." This means that we don't necessarily get to decide what time we want it to be. We can't decide we're going to start parenting when our kids are grown up. If we miss their childhood, we've missed the appointed time to parent.

According to verse 11, eternity is written into our hearts. We long for it even while we can't understand the longing until we know the One who put the longing there.

Discerning the Times

Let's explore together the meaning today of some of what we've just been saying.

9. The premise of this first lesson (first five chapters of the book) is: God created time. He is not subject to or shackled by it in any way. How does understanding this open up a world of possibilities for your present and future?

_____

_____

_____

10. On page 39, Pastor Troy pointed out, "Your view of time is determined by the condition of your heart and the authority you walk in or the victimization you are burdened with." What did he mean by that? Can you think of an example?

11. On pages 54 to 59, Pastor Troy discusses the power of 28. What do insights like this one tell you about the author of God's Word?

12. Review the summary statements on pages 57-59 of *Redeeming Your Timeline*. How many were you able to check? Which ones do you need help with?

_____

_____

_____

_____

_____

Timely Words

Let's get personal about the content of this chapter and the passages from God's Word we have been considering. Some questions may be difficult to address even in a small group, but we need to trust in one another's willingness to honor confidentiality and offer support.

13. As a result of these first five chapters in *Redeeming Your Timeline*, how has your life as a follower of Jesus been challenged?

_____

_____

_____

_____

14. In what specific area of life under the sun do you sense the Holy Spirit urging you to pursue as you seek to redeem your timeline?

_____

_____

_____

_____

_____

Final Matters

A parting review thought from Pastor Troy:

You can be in perfect timing with both your times and your seasons so that all of God's good purposes are fulfilled in your life. Being in sync with God's timing lines you up for a powerful Kingdom advantage.

For He says: "'In an acceptable time I have heard you, and in the day of salvation I have helped you.' Behold, now is the accepted time; behold, now is the day of salvation" (2 Corinthians 6:2).

This study is a time of God's special work in you. Don't miss out.

[As the session winds down, encourage the group to prepare for the next session and be in prayer for each of the other group members.]

Here are some last-minute tasks as we conclude this session:

- Who can you invite to join you in this adventure pursuing greatness? [Discuss who might be good additions to the group.]

- *Redeeming Your Timeline* reading assignment for next week: Chapters 6–10.

- Prayer requests from the group.

Close in prayer.

Daily Follow-Up

Day 1

Read: Ephesians 5:15-16

See then that you walk circumspectly, not as fools but as wise, redeeming the time, because the days are evil.

Respond: As you begin this study, what is your understanding of redeeming the time in evil days in your own life?

_____

_____

_____

_____

_____

Day 2

Read: Psalm 31:15

> *My times are in Your hand; deliver me from the hand of my enemies, and from those who persecute me.*

Respond: In this memory verse for the session, what is David actually saying about God and what is he praying for based on his relationship with God?

_____

_____

_____

_____

Day 3

Read: 1 John 2:17

And the world is passing away, and the lust of it; but he who does the will of God abides forever.

Respond: The world is on the clock and God is the timekeeper. What is your attitude about diligently doing God's will?

_____

_____

_____

_____

Day 4

Read: Luke 4:13 KJV

And when the devil had ended all the temptation, he departed from him for a season.

Respond: Seasons have starting and ending points, after which come other seasons. Jesus wasn't protected for tough seasons. What season are you in right now and how are you experiencing God's presence in that season?

_____

_____

_____

_____

_____

Day 5

Read: Ecclesiastes 3:1

> *To everything there is a season, a time for every purpose under heaven.*

Respond: In what ways are you most aware of time right now? How confident are you that your purposes are lining up with the times you are in?

_____

_____

_____

_____

Day 6

Use the following space to write any thoughts God has put in your heart and mind about the things we have looked at in this session and during your Daily Follow-Up time this week.

_____

_____

_____

_____

_____

_____

_____

_____

_____

_____

_____

If you haven't done so already, make sure to read the assignment for the next session in *Redeeming Your Timeline.*

The Purpose and Function of Time

Memory Verse

So teach us to number our days,
that we may gain a heart of wisdom.
—Psalm 90:12

The band Chicago produced a lot of classic hits and unforgettable lines. In one song they asked, "Does anybody really know what time it is; does anybody really care...about time?" Believers should care. Understanding when and how time started, why we need time, and where we are in the timeline is of utmost importance. We should care about what we are doing with this all-too-brief time that we have. God does want to teach us to count our days and not take them for granted as we develop wisdom from His Word and under His Spirit's guidance.

Redeeming Your Timeline Reading Assignment for This Session

Chapters Six to Ten (pages 63–116)

Preparing

[If the group is new, doesn't know one another, or you have several new folks joining the group this session, you may want to have name tags or take time again to have each person introduce themselves briefly.]

[The questions will always be written as if you are asking them. Feel free to use only some of the questions or alter the wording to fit your style or the group.]

1.   Let's have a report from the group: How many of you have an example in your walk with God this past week that involved thinking differently about time?

_____

_____

_____

_____

_____

2.   Each chapter in *Redeeming Your Timeline* includes a "headline" or summary statement for the teaching. Here are the five from this section:

- **Chapter 6**: Time for humanity begins with the fall of Adam and ends with the last chance of redemption and final act of judgment.

- **Chapter 7**: The clock on humanity began ticking when Adam and Eve rebelled against God and ate the fruit of the Tree of the Knowledge of Good and Evil. They fell from absolute time (redeemed) into relative time (unredeemed) where sin, age, and decay—the Second Law of Thermodynamics—leads to death. Time is the place you fall to because death can be dealt with there, even eliminated, by redemption.

- **Chapter 8:** When you view your timeline, you either see it according to nature without a creator, which is all about history, or you view it as a creation made by our Creator and it's all about destiny.

- **Chapter 9:** Jesus illustrates through the Bible He can travel through time and He can cause others to travel through time with Him. The Word proves He shows up and is manifest in your history as well as your destiny.

- **Chapter 10:** God sees and is interacting with your past and your future right now. He knows you in your entire timeline, all of it, right now.

Which of these chapters left a lasting impression on you? Why?

_____

_____

_____

_____

_____

3. Several times Pastor Troy made the point that Jesus is a time traveler. How does this idea impact your view of the Bible and your understanding of Jesus?

_____

_____

_____

_____

_____

Timeless Words

The following Bible passage connects with the main themes of the assignment in *Redeeming Your Timeline.* Let's hear it read as we follow along, and we will include these verses in our conversation about the book.

[Ask someone to read aloud the passage as the rest of the group follows along.]

Genesis 3:1-7:

¹ Now the serpent was more cunning than any beast of the field which the Lord God had made. And he said to the woman, "Has God indeed said, 'You shall not eat of every tree of the garden'?"

² And the woman said to the serpent, "We may eat the fruit of the trees of the garden;

³ but of the fruit of the tree which is in the midst of the garden, God has said, 'You shall not eat it, nor shall you touch it, lest you die.'"

⁴ Then the serpent said to the woman, "You will not surely die.

⁵ For God knows that in the day you eat of it your eyes will be opened, and you will be like God, knowing good and evil."

⁶ So when the woman saw that the tree was good for food, that it was pleasant to the eyes, and a tree desirable to make one wise, she took of its fruit and ate. She also gave to her husband with her, and he ate.

⁷ Then the eyes of both of them were opened, and they knew that they were naked; and they sewed fig leaves together and made themselves coverings.

4. When this verse says, "Their eyes were opened..." to what extent do you think Adam and Eve's world was changed? How do you think time, space and matter now became curses?

_____

_____

_____

_____

_____

5. How does God's original warning to Adam in Genesis 2:16-17 support the idea that "a day is like a thousand years" to God as we read in Psalms 90:4 and 2 Peter 3:8? (Pages 68-70)

_____

_____

_____

_____

6. In section 2 of the book, we learn that time is both a blessing and a curse. In your understanding, how is time a curse? How is it a blessing from God? (Page 69)

_____

_____

_____

_____

7. Commenting on this passage, Pastor Troy notes, "Getting back to time, time, space, matter, sin, and death are in perfect continuum. One cannot exist without the others. Adam had dominion over time, space, matter, sin, and death until he fell into sin. The day he fell into sin, he was subject to death, which means he was subject to time" (page 68). How does this affect your view of the fall of humanity?

Study Notes

Discerning the Times

Let's explore together the meaning today of some of what we've just been saying.

8.   What was your understanding of the biblical timeline before reading these chapters? How has it changed after reading Pastor Troy's view of the biblical timeline?

9.   Pastor Troy wrote on page 84: What if God created everything—I mean everything—in six days no matter what you want to call a day, here it comes...with history attached to it." What does he mean?

10.   What are some of the observations we can make once we understand that God places a high value on maturity (see pages 84–87)?

Timely Words

Let's get personal about the content of these chapters and the passages from God's Word we have been considering. These questions may be difficult to address even in a small group, but we need to trust in one another's willingness to honor confidentiality and offer support.

11. On pages 106-107, Pastor Troy stepped back for a brief summary of the book so far:

> Before your brain starts smoking, let's rehash some basic steps into this mind-blowing revelation and keep it fresh.
>
> 1. Time is God's way of keeping everything from happening at once. He is the God of order. He wants certain things worked out and accomplished.
>
> 2. Time is created by God for the purpose of redemption.
>
> 3. God is not subject to time or confined by it in any way. He is eternal and rules both time and eternity. He can step into or pull out of any time or place He pleases.
>
> 4. God is with us now in our time frame. He is also with us in our past, in our future, and—this next part is very important—*NOW*.

Related to this outline of the study, how are you being affected by these revelations on time and how it works in your life?

_____

_____

_____

_____

12. How does Pastor Troy's revelation of the train from his "myopic" view as compared to God's "eternal" view change the way you see time? How does it impact the way you understand redemption?

_____

_____

_____

_____

13. On pages 111–113 Pastor Troy provides another checklist for tracking the implications of redeeming your timeline. Read through them as a group and talk together about their significance in a believer's life.

_____

_____

Final Matters

A parting review thought from Pastor Troy:

You do not have to be caged or shackled by your past, no matter how terrible the events you have experienced. Nothing is wasted in the Kingdom and when His Kingdom comes into your timeline, King Jesus brings more than your present life with Him. He also brings a history and a future with Him! (Page 109)

[As the session winds down, encourage the group to prepare for the next session and be in prayer for each of the other group members.]

Here are some last-minute tasks as we conclude this session:

- One way to develop momentum is to continually invite others to join the group. [Discuss who might be good additions to the group.]

- *Redeeming Your Timeline* reading assignment for next week: Chapters 11–14.

- Prayer requests from the group about the need to identify and overcome points of inertia in our lives.

Close in prayer and consider using the prayer on page 114, reading it in unison and then sitting in silence and allowing God's Spirit to confirm what you are learning and deciding.

Daily Follow-Up

Day 1

Read: Revelation 22:13

> *I am Alpha and Omega, the Beginning and the End, the First and the Last.*

Respond: Beyond these terms Jesus uses for Himself, what terms do you use to describe what He means to you?

_____

_____

_____

_____

_____

_____

Day 2

Read: Genesis 2:16-17

And the Lord God commanded the man, saying, "Of every tree of the garden you may freely eat; but of the tree of the knowledge of good and evil you shall not eat, for in the day that you eat of it you shall surely die."

Respond: We all confirm that Adam was our ancestor by our own sins; once time, space, matter, sin and death are unleashed, they cannot be "put back in the box" (Romans 5:12, page 68). How can you look past the curse to thank God for the gift that time is?

_____

_____

_____

_____

Day 3

Read: Romans 6:23

For the wages of sin is death, but the free gift of God is eternal life in Christ Jesus our Lord.

Respond: If eternal life is a free gift, how are you demonstrating to others that you value it highly even though it came to you free?

_____

....

....

....

....

Day 4

Read: Jeremiah 29:11

For I know the thoughts that I think toward you, says the Lord, thoughts of peace and not of evil, to give you a future and a hope.

Respond: What three things does God think toward you? Which of them thrills you the most right now?

....

....

....

....

Day 5

Read: Hebrews 13:8

Jesus Christ is the same yesterday, today, and forever.

Respond: As Pastor Troy points out, Jesus is in each of these time frames *"all at the same time."* How does Jesus always being the same apply when you think about your past, present, and future?

_____

_____

_____

_____

Day 6

Use the following space to write any thoughts God has put in your heart and mind about the things we have looked at in this session and during your Daily Follow-Up time this week.

If you haven't done so already, make sure to read the assignment for the next session in *Redeeming Your Timeline*.

_____

_____

_____

_____

_____

The Redeemer and the Power of Redemption

Memory Verse

*Being justified freely by His grace through
the redemption that is in Christ Jesus.*
—ROMANS 3:24

Because Jesus as God has access to our past, present, and future, what He has accomplished in His life, death, and resurrection makes a difference beyond our full comprehension. His redemption brings benefits that overwhelm us.

Those benefits of redemption include but are not limited to:

- Eternal life (Revelation 5:9-10)

- Forgiveness of sins (Ephesians 1:7)

- Righteousness (Romans 5:17)

- Freedom from the law's curse (Galatians 3:13)

- Freedom from guilt and shame (Romans 3:24)

- Freedom from accusation (John 8:11)

- Complete justification (Romans 3:24)

- Adoption into God's family (Galatians 4:5)

- Deliverance from sin's bondage (Titus 2:14; 1 Peter 1:14-18)

- Peace with God (Colossians 1:18-20)

- The indwelling of the Holy Spirit (1 Corinthians 6:19-20)

All of this and more—in fact, everything takes on new life and meaning in Christ.

Redeeming Your Timeline Reading Assignment for This Session

Chapters 11–14 (pages 117–148)

Preparing

[Acknowledge any newcomers. Consider opening with prayer and focus on what it means to apply the memory verse for the session.]

[The questions are written as if you are asking them. Feel free to use only some of the questions or alter the wording to fit your style or the group.]

1. In your working experience, what's the best benefit you've ever received in a job?

2.   For those who have been with us from the start, how have these sessions and your reading affected the way you think about time?

_____

_____

_____

_____

3. The premise of this session is "Redemption Changes Everything." What are some possible parts of "everything" that we sometimes struggle to believe can be changed?

_____

_____

_____

_____

Timeless Words

The following Bible passage is central to the chapters of *Redeeming Your Timeline* for this session. Let's hear it read as we follow along, and we will include these verses in our conversation about the book.

[Ask someone to read aloud the passage for the group as the rest follow along.]

John 2:1-11:

¹ On the third day there was a wedding in Cana of Galilee, and the mother of Jesus was there.

² Now both Jesus and His disciples were invited to the wedding.

³ And when they ran out of wine, the mother of Jesus said to Him, "They have no wine."

⁴ Jesus said to her, "Woman, what does your concern have to do with Me? My hour has not yet come."

⁵ His mother said to the servants, "Whatever He says to you, do it."

⁶ Now there were set there six waterpots of stone, according to the manner of purification of the Jews, containing twenty or thirty gallons apiece.

⁷ Jesus said to them, "Fill the waterpots with water." And they filled them up to the brim.

⁸ And He said to them, "Draw some out now, and take it to the master of the feast." And they took it.

⁹ When the master of the feast had tasted the water that was made wine, and did not know where it came from (but the servants who had drawn the water knew), the master of the feast called the bridegroom.

¹⁰ And he said to him, "Every man at the beginning sets out the good wine, and when the guests have well drunk, then the inferior. You have kept the good wine until now!"

¹¹ This beginning of signs Jesus did in Cana of Galilee, and manifested His glory; and His disciples believed in Him.

4.   What observations can you make about the relationship between Jesus and His mother from this episode? How does turning water to wine speak of Jesus being the master of time? How does it relate to the continuum of space, time, and matter?

_____

_____

_____

_____

5.   In what different ways does timing or time have a significant effect in this passage? For example: *"hour"* (verse 4), *"water that was made wine"* (verse 9), *"beginning"* (verses 10-11).

_____

_____

6. In discussing the implications of this miracle, Pastor Troy noted on page 136: "When Jesus changes the timing of things, He does it for the sake of relationship, and it changes the natural order of timing into a redeemed state. These miracles of redemption are always for the benefit of those in relationship with Him." What does he mean and can you think of other examples from Jesus' life?

7. Before they became containers for very fine wine, what were those stone jugs used for (see verse 6). How did Jesus' miracle redeem those containers for a new purpose? And what is the redemptive lesson He taught with His action?

Study Notes

(verse 4). Just as He did in Luke 2:51, Jesus had to gently remind His own mother that He had higher priorities that determined what He did and when He did it.

(verse 4). Jesus' hour always refers to the ultimate purpose for His time on earth, the costly moment of redemption on the cross. All His words and actions up to that moment pointed to His unique worthiness to bring about redemption.

(verse 10). Jesus didn't just replace the missing wine; He gave it a noticeable upgrade.

Discerning the Times

Let's explore together the meaning today of some of what we've just been studying.

8.   Hopefully you have been taking a few minutes at the end of each chapter to ponder the questions included there (pages 126, 132, 138, 147-148). Which if any of those questions have provoked significant response in you?

_____

_____

_____

_____

9. On page 120, Pastor Troy wrote, "Why would the Lord specifically remove our sins and throw them as far as the east is from the west—a picture of eternal separation? Because He wants them removed completely so we cannot pick them back up again. When Jesus removes them, He removes them for all time and space.

"There is nothing created that redemption doesn't change. Redemption is what happens when Jesus steps onto any scene and has His amazing way. It's what He brings every time to everything in time." What are we saying to Jesus when we try to hang on to old sins or even try to go back and pick them up again?

_____

_____

_____

_____

10. In His first sermon (Luke 4:16-22) Jesus applied a number of significant actions to His work of redemption, using Isaiah 61 as His source. Pastor Troy outlined Jesus' claims on page 123:

1. Reach the poor—people who had never been granted access—with redemption.

2. Heal the brokenhearted—bring hope and love of life to people who had been broken—with redemption.

3. Set captives free by redemption.

4. Restore sight and understanding to the blind by redemption.

5. Set people free from what beat them up: "to set at liberty them that are bruised." Bruised is when you are beat up on the inside, and wounded is when you are beat up on the outside. All this by paying a price only He could pay.

How do these categories push out the boundaries of what we usually think of when we use the term *redemption*?

_____

_____

_____

_____

_____

Timely Words

Let's get personal about the content of these chapters and the passages from God's Word we have been considering. These questions may be difficult to address even in a small group, but we need to trust in one another's willingness to honor confidentiality and offer support.

11. How did you respond to Pastor Troy's comment on page 140: "If you are a believer, your spirit is 100 percent redeemed, your mind is in the process of being redeemed, and your body someday will be redeemed. The reason the funeral business is booming is because our bodies are not yet redeemed"?

_____

_____

_____

_____

12. In what ways have you experienced the truth of the following statement from page 143: "Being born again is the foundation of our faith. *'Being born again, not of corruptible seed, but of incorruptible, by the word of God, which liveth and abideth forever'* (1 Peter 1:23 KJV). Faith in Jesus brings His redemption into our lives and conquers sin and death upon our behalf. Now Jesus has dominion over us and death no longer does"?

_____

_____

13. Which of the bullet points about redemption on pages 144-146 do you think will leave the most lasting impression on your life?

Final Matters

A parting review thought from Pastor Troy:

Your faith is your supernatural key, giving you the open door you need for redemption.

The *physical location and condition* you are in does not limit your ability to find redemption.

The *when* of your timeline does not limit your ability to find redemption.

The *what* of your condition has no determination if redemption can find you and change everything.

REDEEMING YOUR TIMELINE STUDY GUIDE

I could go on and on, but the bottom line is this: you don't consult your time, your place, or your circumstances to see if you can access redemption. You find your faith.

[As the session winds down, encourage the group to prepare for the next session and be in prayer for each of the other group members.]

Here are some last-minute tasks as we conclude this session:

- *Redeeming Your Timeline* reading assignment for next week: Chapters 15–16. Take a few minutes to review the book to this point.

- If you are not already doing so, begin to ask God for a vision that allows you to see the next step beyond your immediate circumstances that He wants you to take with trust in Him regarding your timeline.

- Other prayer requests from the group.

Close in prayer.

Daily Follow-Up

Day 1

Read: Psalm 103:2

Bless the Lord, O my soul, and forget not all His benefits.

Respond: Today, meditate on the benefits you have because of Jesus. Which one tastes sweetest in your soul right now?

_____

_____

_____

_____

Day 2

Read: Romans 3:24

Being justified freely by His grace through the redemption that is in Christ Jesus.

Respond: Understanding that Jesus is a time traveler who likes to rewrite your history, what does "grace through the redemption that is in Christ Jesus" mean to you now?

_____

_____

_____

Day 3

Read: Matthew 9:3-5

And at once some of the scribes said within themselves, "This Man blasphemes!"

But Jesus, knowing their thoughts, said, "Why do you think evil in your hearts? For which is easier, to say, 'Your sins are forgiven you,' or to say, 'Arise and walk'?"

Respond: How is the forgiveness of sins a picture of redeeming time? How about miraculous physical healing? Can that also be a picture of redeeming time? How so?

Day 4

Read: Romans 8:21-23

Because the creation itself also will be delivered from the bondage of corruption into the glorious liberty of the children of God. For we know that the whole creation groans and labors with birth pangs together until now. Not only that, but we also who have the firstfruits of the Spirit, even we ourselves groan within ourselves, eagerly waiting for the adoption, the redemption of our body.

Respond: In the next five minutes think about some of the places in your past you would like to see redeemed. Write them down. How would that change your today?

_____

_____

_____

_____

_____

Day 5

Read: Ephesians 2:8 (NIV)

For it is by grace [the power of God] *you have been saved* [redeemed], *through faith* [believing and trusting in Him]— *and this is not from yourselves, it is the gift of God.*

Respond: Take a few minutes and express your gratitude to God for His free gift of salvation to you in Jesus Christ.

_____

_____

_____

_____

Day 6

Use the following space to write any thoughts God has put in your heart and mind about the things we have looked at in this session and during your Daily Follow-Up time this week.

If you haven't done so already, make sure to read the assignment for the next session in *Redeeming Your Timeline*.

_____

_____

_____

_____

_____

Redeeming the Times of Your Life

Memory Verse

*Let the redeemed of the Lord say so, whom He
has redeemed from the hand of the enemy.*
—Psalm 107:2

God always goes ahead of us and always makes the way, but that still means we have to follow and step out. God is never in a hurry, but that doesn't mean He can say it and have it happen, as in "Let there be light." *Redeeming Your Timeline* means being willing to welcome Jesus anywhere in your past present, and future. It means seeing and experiencing God's freeing redemption and saying so to those around us.

Redeeming Your Timeline Reading Assignment for This Session

Chapters 15 through 16 (pages 149–168)

Preparing

[Open with prayer.]

[Now that you have been meeting for four weeks, consider warming up by encouraging the group to share experiences related to the chapters they have read for this session.]

1. What do the terms "quick change" and "slow change" mean to you now that you have been thinking about God's access to your timeline?

2. If you could go back in time (like the Lord actually can), what two or three events come to mind where God's redeeming work could make a difference?

3. As a review, Pastor Troy listed the first four premises of this book on pages 151-152. Take some time as a group to discuss each one briefly and make sure you understand the point related to Jesus' sovereignty over time, space, and matter.

Timeless Words

The following Bible passage is central to the fifteenth to sixteenth chapters of *Redeeming Your Timeline*. Let's hear it read as we follow along, and we will include these verses in our conversation about the book.

> [Ask several people to read aloud the passage for the group as the rest follow along.]

John 11:1-7, 17-44:

> *¹ Now a certain man was sick, Lazarus of Bethany, the town of Mary and her sister Martha. ² It was that Mary who anointed the Lord with fragrant oil and wiped His feet with her hair, whose brother Lazarus was sick. ³ Therefore the sisters sent to Him, saying, "Lord, behold, he whom You love is sick."*

⁴ When Jesus heard that, He said, "This sickness is not unto death, but for the glory of God, that the Son of God may be glorified through it." ⁵ Now Jesus loved Martha and her sister and Lazarus. ⁶ So, when He heard that he was sick, He stayed two more days in the place where He was. ⁷ Then after this He said to the disciples, "Let us go to Judea again."

¹⁷ So when Jesus came, He found that he had already been in the tomb four days. ¹⁸ Now Bethany was near Jerusalem, about two miles away. ¹⁹ And many of the Jews had joined the women around Martha and Mary, to comfort them concerning their brother.

²⁰ Then Martha, as soon as she heard that Jesus was coming, went and met Him, but Mary was sitting in the house. ²¹ Then Martha said to Jesus, "Lord, if You had been here, my brother would not have died. ²² But even now I know that whatever You ask of God, God will give You."

²³ Jesus said to her, "Your brother will rise again."

²⁴ Martha said to Him, "I know that he will rise again in the resurrection at the last day."

²⁵ Jesus said to her, "I am the resurrection and the life. He who believes in Me, though he may die, he shall live. ²⁶ And whoever lives and believes in Me shall never die. Do you believe this?"

27 She said to Him, "Yes, Lord, I believe that You are the Christ, the Son of God, who is to come into the world." 28 And when she had said these things, she went her way and secretly called Mary her sister, saying, "The Teacher has come and is calling for you." 29 As soon as she heard that, she arose quickly and came to Him.

30 Now Jesus had not yet come into the town, but was in the place where Martha met Him.

31 Then the Jews who were with her in the house, and comforting her, when they saw that Mary rose up quickly and went out, followed her, saying, "She is going to the tomb to weep there." 32 Then, when Mary came where Jesus was, and saw Him, she fell down at His feet, saying to Him, "Lord, if You had been here, my brother would not have died."

33 Therefore, when Jesus saw her weeping, and the Jews who came with her weeping, He groaned in the spirit and was troubled. 34 And He said, "Where have you laid him?" They said to Him, "Lord, come and see." 35 Jesus wept.

36 Then the Jews said, "See how He loved him!" 37 And some of them said, "Could not this Man, who opened the eyes of the blind, also have kept this man from dying?"

38 Then Jesus, again groaning in Himself, came to the tomb. It was a cave, and a stone lay against it. 39 Jesus said, "Take away the stone." Martha, the sister of him who was dead, said to Him, "Lord, by this time there is a stench, for he has been dead four days." ⁴⁰ Jesus said to her, "Did I not say to you that if you would believe you would see the glory of God?"

⁴¹ Then they took away the stone from the place where the dead man was lying. And Jesus lifted up His eyes and said, "Father, I thank You that You have heard Me. ⁴² And I know that You always hear Me, but because of the people who are standing by I said this, that they may believe that You sent Me." ⁴³ Now when He had said these things, He cried with a loud voice, "Lazarus, come forth!"

⁴⁴ And he who had died came out bound hand and foot with graveclothes, and his face was wrapped with a cloth. Jesus said to them, "Loose him, and let him go."

4. What was the relationship between Jesus and each of the people in this biblical account? Why is relationship important to redeeming time? What guided Jesus' decision not to immediately rush to Lazarus' sickbed?

_____

_____

_____

_____

_____

5.   To review, *Premise 4* states: "You can introduce redemption into any part of your timeline and it changes everything within the timeline including space and matter." How does this episode with Jesus demonstrate this premise? How do Jesus' words in verse 4 fit into this premise?

6.   Look again at the point in the events when Scripture records that *"Jesus wept"* (verse 35). Which of the following explanations makes the most sense to you? Why?

- Jesus wept in sympathy with the sisters and the crowd.

- Jesus wept in sadness that He had waited too long to heal Lazarus.

- Jesus wept because His friend Lazarus would now have to die twice in his lifetime.

▪ Jesus wept over the massive tidal wave of unbelief that He knew could only be effectively confronted by His own death and resurrection.

7.   Take a few minutes to imagine what happened in Bethany now that the time of mourning has been suddenly changed into a time of rejoicing. What was Jesus' promise to us in verses 25-26? Note Pastor Troy's comment: "Jesus was saying, *'It's not about a day. It's about Me!* I Am greater than any measure of time whether it was four days ago when Lazarus died or thousands of years in the future when he rises out of the ground. I Am the resurrection. I Am life, and I Am what you are waiting for. Not a day. Not a year. You are waiting for Me to step into time—and I Am here, right now!'" (Page 162)

Study Notes

(verse 3). The sisters didn't tell Jesus anything He didn't know and they refrained from telling Jesus what He should do. But they assumed He would come quickly. It's actually possible that Lazarus was dead by the time the messengers found Him.

(verse 4). One of the hardest lessons to accept is when God refuses to answer on our timetable. We only succeed in trying to limit Him.

(verse 26). Martha needed to upgrade her belief system. She knew Jesus had authority over sickness; she wasn't sure about death.

(verse 41b). This prayer makes it clear that Jesus was speaking out loud what He had already gotten permission to do from God the Father.

(verse 43). Imagine what would have happened if Jesus hadn't deliberately limited His command to Lazarus!

Discerning the Times

Let's explore together the meaning today of some of what we've just been saying.

8.   What would it mean to invite Jesus into the dark or shameful places of our past? What difference can He make?

9. What difference does it make when we stop looking at the past as a closed book instead of a place Jesus can easily visit and transform? Take into account Pastor Troy's comment based on Joshua 3:16. (Page 152)

> I am not saying those things are no big deal. I am also not saying you can go back into time and change that; but my friend, I have great news. *Jesus is a time traveler.* He is not subject to time. I am saying He can bring redemption into that moment and it will change the curse to a blessing, right now. It's like backing up the flow of the curse that prohibits you from crossing into your promised places—all the way back to Adam or the point of origin! (Pages 153-154)

[Review the Section 3 summary on pages 163-165 and encourage the group to make comments about the points listed on those pages.]

Timely Words

Let's get personal about the content of these chapters and the passages from God's Word we have been considering. These questions may be difficult to address even in a small group, but we need to trust in one another's willingness to honor confidentiality and offer support.

10. Read Psalms 139:7-9 in the Passion Translation from page 149. Do you see the references to time throughout? What do you think of Pastor Troy's conclusion that Jesus is actually waiting for you to discover that He actually wants to redeem your past?

_____

_____

_____

_____

11. How is Jesus' access to the times and places in your past a source of hope you didn't have before? What's the difference between confessing past sin and letting Jesus redeem past sin?

_____

_____

_____

12. Take some time to reflect on and pray the prayer Pastor Troy included on page 166. After reading through it, read it again to the Lord out loud. Then sit quietly for as long as necessary and let Him minister to your past, present, and future.

Final Matters

A parting review thought from Pastor Troy:

> We have spent sixteen chapters taking a deep look into the reality of how God interacts with time and how we can invite Jesus to bring His redeeming power to change everything.
>
> You can simply invite His visible awesomeness, glory, or manifest presence into any non-redeemed place in your timeline. If you see Him there in that place, you will see a curse change to a blessing. You will instantly see what flows from that past place into your right now place is life instead of death. A river of life in the river of time.

[As the session winds down, encourage the group to prepare for the next session and be in prayer for each of the other group members.]

Here are some last-minute tasks as we conclude this session:

- In what ways do you think God has been speaking to you through these sessions up to this point?

- *Redeeming Your Timeline* reading assignment for next week: Chapters 17 to 24.

- Prayer requests from the group.

Close in prayer.

Daily Follow-Up

Day 1

Read: John 11:25-26

I am the resurrection and the life. He who believes in Me, though he may die, he shall live. And whoever lives and believes in Me shall never die. Do you believe this?

Respond: Have you ever really answered the question Jesus asked Martha at the end of that statement above? How does it relate to your timeline?

Day 2

Read: Psalm 34:8

Oh, taste and see that the Lord is good!

Respond: How would you illustrate the truth of this verse from your own life?

_____

_____

_____

_____

Day 3

Read: Mark 2:27-28 (NIV)

Then He said to them, "The Sabbath was made for man, not man for the Sabbath. So the Son of Man is Lord even of the Sabbath."

Respond: The Sabbath is a weekly time marker that points to God and His gift of time. How do you use the day of rest as a way of acknowledging God's gift?

_____

_____

....

....

....

Day 4

Read: Revelation 5:10 (NIV)

You have made them to be a kingdom and priests to serve our God, and they will reign on the earth.

Respond: In what ways do you see yourself as a citizen of God's kingdom with authority to minister as a priest to serve Him in the world?

....

....

....

....

Day 5

Read: Psalm 107:2

Let the redeemed of the Lord say so, whom He has redeemed from the hand of the enemy.

Respond: How have you been putting redeeming time into practice in your life? How have you seen the redemption of God deliver you from the hand of the enemy in that place?

_____

_____

_____

_____

Day 6

Use the following space to write any thoughts God has put in your heart and mind about the things we have looked at in this session and during your Daily Follow-Up time this week.

If you haven't done so already, make sure to read the assignment for the next session in *Redeeming Your Timeline*.

_____

_____

_____

_____

Session Five

Being a King and a Priest of Your Time

Memory Verse

To Him [Jesus Christ] *who loved us and washed us from our sins in His own blood, and has made us kings and priests to His God and Father, to Him be glory and dominion forever and ever. Amen.*
—Revelation 1:5-6

In the opening verses of Revelation, John is writing after having seen all that the Holy Spirit will reveal through his pen in the book of the Revelation of Jesus Christ. He has already heard the saints in eternity sing the new song that includes lyrics about our future role as kings and priests. This picture is confirmed by Peter in First Peter 2:5: ***"You also, as living stones, are being built up a spiritual house, a holy priesthood, to offer up spiritual sacrifices acceptable to God through Jesus Christ"*** (see also verse 9). Isn't it time we start living out our redemption?

Redeeming Your Timeline Reading Assignment for This Session

Chapters 17 to 24 (pages 169–236)

Preparing

[Open with prayer.]

[Consider warming up by encouraging the group to share experiences related to the chapters they have read for this session.]

1.   Which of the amazing stories in these chapters did you like the best? Why?

_____

_____

_____

_____

2.   From Pastor Troy's stories, how would you explain to someone the possibility of inviting Jesus into their past for healing? What should they expect to see happen? Consider Isaiah 1:18 and the "un-dyeing" of the red cloth (page 122).

_____

_____

_____

_____

3.   At this end point in the study, what principle or insight do you think will have a long-term effect on the way you live the Christian life?

_____

_____

Timeless Words

The following Bible passage is central to the seventeenth to twenty-fourth chapters of *Redeeming Your Timeline*. Let's hear it read as we follow along, and we will include these verses in our conversation about the book.

[Ask someone to read aloud the passage for the group as the rest follow along.]

Psalm 103:10-14:

[10] *He has not dealt with us according to our sins, Nor punished us according to our iniquities.*

[11] *For as the heavens are high above the earth, So great is His mercy toward those who fear Him;*

[12] *As far as the east is from the west, So far has He removed our transgressions from us.*

[13] *As a father pities his children, So, the Lord pities those who fear Him.*

¹⁴ For He knows our frame; [our time frame too] He remembers that we are dust.

4.   In light of this study, do you see this passage from pages 215-216 as a beautiful picture of redeeming time? How so? Explain why the the Lord chose to remove our sins "as far as the east is from the west." Why not the north and the south (page 120)?

_____

_____

_____

_____

_____

5.   What do you think the psalmist meant when he penned "For as the heavens are high above the earth, so great is His mercy toward those who fear him"? Could he be seeing his own life from the view above just like Pastor Troy did in his vision above the train (pages 103-105)?

_____

_____

_____

_____

6. According to this Psalm, why is God such a redemption freak?

_____

_____

_____

_____

7. Refer to Luke 17:15-19 on page 194 in the book. Jesus "healed" or "cleansed" all ten of the lepers, but one took the extra time and effort to return and thank Him. His grateful heart brought a huge upgrade. What was it and how can you tap into upgrades in redeeming your timeline?

_____

_____

_____

_____

Study Notes

God's word on time and redemption is so rich, especially when viewed through the lens of personal experience. Relationship is everything when it comes to understanding God's character through His word. The practice of redeeming your timeline for supernatural skillsets for healing past wounds, calming future anxieties and discovering rest right now is all about relationship. If you understand God is good and He loves you, you will discover He wants to invest in your future by healing your past. Do you see that God, like a good father, loves restoration over punishment?

Discerning the Times

Let's explore together the meaning today of some of what we've just been saying.

8. As a group, discuss the eight statements of Biblical truth Pastor Troy included in Chapter 20. How are you and I personally responsible for our past, present, and future? What points exposed an attitude you need to confront in order to practice redeeming your timeline?

_____

_____

_____

_____

9. In Chapter 22, Pastor Troy included seven areas of life that should be considered when praying over needed redemption in our past. Discuss these as a group and note ones that suggest God is speaking to you personally. They are:

1. Redeeming the times of wasted years or lost investment.

2. Redeeming a time of great failure.

3. Redeeming a time of bondage.

4. Redeeming a time of great injustice.

5. Redeeming times when you were absent for people you should have been there for and vice versa.

6. Redeeming times of lost opportunity.

7. Redeeming the time of family in times way past.

Timely Words

Let's get personal about the content of this chapter and the passages from God's Word we have been considering. These questions may be difficult to address even in a small group, but we need to trust in one another's willingness to honor confidentiality and offer support.

10. Pastor Troy challenged each of us on page 196 with this statement: "When Jesus invites you into a redeemed place, you have to be willing to change your garments from sackcloth to praise. You have to be willing to live according to a different experience. It is one thing for God to reveal to you His new plan, it's a whole other thing for you to conform your life to the image of that plan." What does it mean to you? How does it relate to redeeming your timeline?

_____

_____

_____

11. On pages 208-210, Pastor Troy has included a sample prayer for inviting Jesus to redeem a past event as only He can. Take enough time to listen to the Holy Spirit bring to mind things from your own past that could benefit from His redemption. Now use the prayer to practice letting Jesus remix your past with His power.

_____

_____

_____

_____

12. On page 229, Pastor Troy issued this invitation: "Ask Jesus to visit you on your last day and make your last minutes glorify Him. You don't have to wait for that day to ask Him to be there (see John 21:19)." Why would this be an important thing to do? Why do you want to finish well?

[If the group has been prepared by the Holy Spirit to act decisively and personally regarding the teaching in _Redeeming Your Timeline_, lead them through this last question.]

On page 181, Pastor Troy counseled from his own experience, "When you bring the manifest Redeemer into a tragic or terrible time, what flows from that time forward is redemption. I will continue to reap the benefits of redemption from that once terrible and tragic hour, all the days of my life. I would not be surprised if I still have a number-one hit song yet to be manifest." Have you found the Holy Spirit whispering into your soul about an area or experience from your past that He wants to visit with redemption? If you're ready, see the steps below. Take time individually and as a group to respond to these steps.

Activating Redemption into Your Time Frames

So here is what you do:

1. Ask the Holy Spirit to search your heart and your entire time-line. Give Him full disclosure of your life—the good, the bad, the ugly, the grand—all of it. (See Scriptures on searching the times in your life in Section Five.)

2. There will be certain markers within your life where you still experience terrible loss and pain. These are the places you are going to invite the Lord Jesus Christ to be made manifest in that unredeemed epic event or that season. (See Scriptures on identifying markers and places that need redemption in Section Five.)

3. Invite God into that place. Repent and ask Him to have total dominion in that very place. Ask the Lord to show you His

presence in that place. Finding Jesus there will change everything for you. (See Scriptures on inviting His manifest presence and glory into your space-time in Section Five.)

4. Claim and declare your redemption. (See Scriptures on declarations and redemption in Section Five.)

5. Commit your life to living from victory in that place because of the blood of the Lamb and the power of redemption. (See Scriptures on vows, commitment to victory, and redemption in Section Five.)

6. Celebrate your freedom and make a big deal out of your change. Note the changes that happen in you now because of the redemption Jesus has brought to that place in time. (See Scriptures on seeing the new thing, acknowledging the Lord, and the prophetic acts of celebration in Section Five.)

7. Live a prophetic and victorious lifestyle dedicated to the contemplation and the celebration of redemption. (See Chapter 20 on stewarding the impact and managing the change of redeeming time.)

Final Matters

A parting review thought from Pastor Troy:

Bringing the King's redemption into your "right now" time is all about connecting with His manifest presence in every moment. Even in the places where He is hidden throughout your day, He is with you. Jesus is just as present when He is hidden as when He is clearly seen.

And lo, I am with you always, even to the end of the age (Matthew 28:20).

Even if you can't detect the hand of God, you can always go after the heart of God:

The Lord hath sought him a man after his own heart, and the Lord hath commanded him to be captain over his people (1 Samuel 13:14 KJV).

Learning to live a life of full disclosure before God and saying, "Here I am. All of me," is how you bring redemption into every "right now." Recommitting your life to be available to God's presence is everything when it comes to redeeming present time.

[As this final session winds down, encourage the group to be in prayer for each of the other group members in the weeks to come, that God will help them see His redeeming work in their lives.]

Here are some last-minute tasks as we conclude this session:

- What opportunities for helping others to redeem their timelines are available through your church or that the rest of the group might know about?

[Encourage group members to describe places and opportunities they have discovered to help others in this process.]

- *Redeeming Your Timeline* reading assignment for next week: Throughout this week, review the contents of the book to highlight the lessons you have learned along the way. Be watchful of the way Jesus is doing His redeeming work in your life. Keep the various applicable Scripture passages in the final section of the book close at hand for reference as the Spirit works to lead you in redeeming various parts of your life.

- Prayer requests from the group.

Close in prayer.

Daily Follow-Up

Day 1

Read: Psalm 34:8

> *Oh, taste and see that the Lord is good; blessed is the man who trusts in Him.*

Respond: In what ways are you experiencing the goodness of the Lord as you consider His redeeming work in your past, present, and future?

_____

_____

_____

_____

_____

Day 2

Read: 1 Samuel 13:14b

> *The Lord has sought for Himself a man after His own heart, and the Lord has commanded him to be commander over His people.*

Respond: God read the heart of David, the man who prayed "Create in me a clean heart, O God" and knew David's heart was in the right place, despite sin's stumbles and disasters. What does God read in your heart?

_____

_____

_____

_____

Day 3

Read: Psalm 39:4

Lord, make me to know my end, and what is the measure of my days, that I may know how frail I am.

Respond: If you have a struggle trusting God to redeem your future, read again the prayer on page 114 and use it to express yourself to the Lord.

_____

_____

_____

_____

Day 4

Read: 1 John 3:2

> *But we know that when He is revealed, we shall be like Him, for we shall see Him as He is.*

Respond: How does this verse inform you about God's plans for your future? What is your response?

....

....

....

....

....

Day 5

Read: Revelation 1:5-6

> *To Him [Jesus Christ] who loved us and washed us from our sins in His own blood, ⁶ and has made us kings and priests to His God and Father, to Him be glory and dominion forever and ever. Amen.*

Respond: The memory verse for this week has been a great picture of how God wants us to participate in His Kingdom. What are you doing to live as a king and priest?

_____

_____

_____

_____

_____

Day 6

Use the following space to write any thoughts God has put in your heart and mind about the things we have looked at in this session and during your Daily Follow-Up time this week.

_____

_____

_____

_____

_____

_____

Small Group and Leader Helps

Resources to make your small group experience even better!

Frequently Asked Questions about Small Groups

What do we do on the *first night of our group?*

Like all fun things in life—have a party! A "get to know you" coffee, dinner, or dessert is a great way to launch a new study. You may want to review the Group Agreement (pages 115-117) and share the names of a few friends you can invite to join you. But most importantly, have fun before your study time begins.

Where do we *find new members for our group?*

This can be troubling, especially for new groups that have only a few people or for existing groups that lose a few people along the way. We encourage you to pray with your group and then brainstorm a list of people from work, church, your neighborhood, your children's school, family, the gym, and so forth. Then have each group member invite several of the people on his or her list. Another good strategy is to ask church leaders to make an announcement or allow a bulletin insert.

No matter how you find members, it's vital that you stay on the lookout for new people to join your group. All groups tend to go through healthy attrition—the result of moves, releasing new leaders, ministry opportunities, and so forth—and if the group gets too small, it could be at risk of shutting down. If you and your group stay open, you'll be amazed at the people God sends your way. The next person just might become a friend for life. You never know!

How long will this group meet?

Most groups meet weekly for at least their first six weeks, but every other week can work as well. We strongly recommend that the group meet for the first six months on a weekly basis if at all possible. This allows for continuity, and if people miss a meeting they aren't gone for a whole month.

At the end of this study, each group member may decide if he or she wants to continue on for another study. Some groups launch relationships for years to come, and others are stepping-stones into another group experience. Either way, enjoy the journey.

Can we do this study on our own?

Absolutely! This may sound crazy, but one of the best ways to do this study is not with a full house but with a few friends. You may choose to gather with another couple who would enjoy some relational time (perhaps going to the movies or having a quiet dinner) and then walking through this study. Jesus will be with you even if there are only two of you (Matthew 18:20).

What if this group is not working for us?

You're not alone! This could be the result of a personality conflict, life stage difference, geographical distance, level of spiritual maturity, or any number of things. Relax. Pray for God's direction, and at the end of this six-week study, decide whether to continue with this group or find another. You don't typically buy the first car you look at or marry the first person you date, and the same goes with a group. However, don't bail out before the six weeks are up—God might have something to teach you. Also, don't run from conflict or prejudge people before you have given them a chance. God is still working in your life too!

Who is the leader?

Most groups have an official leader. But ideally, the group will mature and members will rotate the leadership of meetings. We have discovered that healthy groups rotate hosts/leaders and homes on a regular basis. This model ensures that all members grow, give their unique contribution, and develop their gifts. This study guide and the Holy Spirit can keep things on track even when you rotate leaders. Christ has promised to be in your midst as you gather. Ultimately, God is your leader each step of the way.

How do we handle the childcare needs in our group?

Very carefully. Seriously, this can be a sensitive issue. We suggest that you empower the group to openly brainstorm solutions. You may try one option that works for a while and then adjust over time. Our favorite approach is for adults to meet in the living room or dining room and to share the cost of a babysitter (or two) who can watch the kids in a different part of the house.

This way, parents don't have to be away from their children all evening when their children are too young to be left at home. A second option is to use one home for the kids and a second home (close by or a phone call away) for the adults. A third idea is to rotate the responsibility of providing a lesson or care for the children either in the same home or in another home nearby. This can be an incredible blessing for kids. Finally, the most common solution is to decide that you need to have a night to invest in your spiritual lives individually or as a couple and to make your own arrangements for childcare. No matter what decision the group makes, the best approach is to dialogue openly about both the problem and the solution.

Small Group Agreement

Our Purpose

To provide a predictable environment where participants experience authentic community and spiritual growth.

Our Values

Group Attendance

> To give priority to the group meeting. We will call or email if we will be late or absent. (Completing the Group Calendar on page 118 will minimize this issue.)

Safe Environment

To help create a safe place where people can be heard and feel loved. (Please, no quick answers, snap judgments, or simple fixes.)

Respect Differences

To be gentle and gracious to fellow group members with different spiritual maturity, personal opinions, temperaments, or "imperfections." We are all works in progress.

Confidentiality

To keep anything that is shared strictly confidential and within the group, and to avoid sharing improper information about those outside the group.

Encouragement for Growth

To be not just takers but givers of life. We want to spiritually multiply our life by serving others with our God-given gifts.

Shared Ownership

To remember that every member is a minister and to ensure that each attender will share a small team role or responsibility over time.

Rotating Hosts/Leaders and Homes

To encourage different people to host the group in their homes and to rotate the responsibility of facilitating each meeting. (See the Group Calendar on page 118.)

Our Expectations

- Refreshments/mealtimes _____
  _____

- Childcare _____
  _____

- When we will meet (day of week) _____

- Where we will meet (place) _____
  _____

- We will begin at (time) _____ and end at _____

- We will do our best to have some or all of us attend a worship service together.
  Our primary worship service time will be _____

- Date of this agreement _____

- Date we will review this agreement again _____

- Who (other than the leader) will review this agreement at the end of this
  _____ study _____

Small Group Calendar

Planning and calendaring can help ensure the greatest participation at every meeting. At the end of each meeting, review this calendar. Be sure to include a regular rotation of host homes and leaders, and don't forget birthdays, socials, church events, holidays, and mission/ministry projects.

Date	Lesson	Host Home	Dessert/Meal	Leader

Memory Verse Cards

Session One

My times are in Your hand; deliver me from the hand of my enemies, and from those who persecute me.

—Psalm 31:15

Session Two

So, teach us to number our days, that we may gain a heart of wisdom.

—Psalm 90:12

Session Three

Being justified freely by His grace through the redemption that is in Christ Jesus.

—Romans 3:24

Session Four

Let the redeemed of the Lord say so, whom He has redeemed from the hand of the enemy.

—PSALM 107:2

Session Five

To Him [Jesus Christ] who loved us and washed us from our sins in His own blood, and has made us kings and priests to His God and Father, to Him be glory and dominion forever and ever. Amen.

—REVELATION 1:5-6

Prayer and Praise Report

SESSION ONE
Prayer Requests
Praise Requests

SESSION TWO

Prayer Requests

Praise Requests

SESSION THREE

Prayer Requests

Praise Requests

SESSION FOUR

Prayer Requests

Praise Requests

SESSION FIVE

Prayer Requests

Praise Requests

Small Group Roster

Name	Email	Phone #

Hosting a Group Gathering

If you're starting a new group, try planning an "open house" before your first formal group meeting. Even if you have only two to four core members, it's a great way to break the ice and to consider prayerfully who else might be open to joining you over the next few weeks. You can also use this kick-off meeting to hand out study guides, spend some time getting to know each other, discuss each person's expectations for the group, and briefly pray for each other. A simple meal or good dessert always makes a kick-off meeting more fun.

After people introduce themselves and share how they ended up being at the meeting (you can play a game to see who has the wildest story!), have everyone respond to a few icebreaker questions:

- What is your favorite family vacation?

- What is one thing you love about your church/our community?

- What are three things about your life growing up that most people here don't know?

Next, ask everyone to tell what he or she hopes to get out of the study. You might want to review the Small Group Agreement and talk about each person's expectations and priorities.

Finally, set an open chair (maybe two) in the center of your group and explain that it represents someone who would enjoy or benefit from this group but who isn't here yet. Ask people to pray about inviting someone to join the group over the next few weeks. Hand out postcards and have everyone write an invitation or two. Don't worry about ending up with too many people; you can always have one discussion circle in the living room and another in the dining room after you watch the lesson. Each group could then report prayer requests and progress at the end of the session.

You can skip this kick-off meeting if your time is limited, but you'll experience a huge benefit if you take the time to connect with each other in this way.

Facilitating a Group for the First Time

- **Sweaty palms are a healthy sign.** The Bible says God is gracious to the humble. Remember who is in control; the time to worry is when you're not worried. Those who are soft in heart (and sweaty palmed) are those whom God is sure to speak through.

- **Seek support.** Ask your leader, co-leader, or close friend to pray for you and prepare with you before the session. Walking through the study will help you anticipate potentially difficult questions and discussion topics.

- **Bring your uniqueness to the study.** Lean into who you are and how God wants you to uniquely lead the study.

- **Prepare. Prepare. Prepare.** Go through the session several times. Consider writing in a journal or fasting for a day to prepare yourself for what God wants to do. **Don't wait until the last minute to prepare.**

- **Ask for feedback so you can grow.** Perhaps in an email or on cards handed out at the study, have everyone write down three things you did well and one thing you could improve on. Don't get defensive. Instead, show an openness to learn and grow.

- **Prayerfully consider launching a new group.** This doesn't need to happen overnight, but God's heart is for this to take place over time. Not all Christians are called to be leaders or teachers, but we are all called to be "shepherds" of a few someday.

- **Share with your group what God is doing in your heart.** God is searching for those whose hearts are fully His. Share your trials and victories. We promise that people will relate.

- **Prayerfully consider whom you would like to pass the baton to next week.** It's only fair. God is ready for the next member of your group to go on the faith journey you just traveled. Make it fun, and expect God to do the rest.

Leadership Training 101

Congratulations! You have responded to the call to help shepherd Jesus' flock. There are few other tasks in the family of God that surpass the contribution you will be making. As you prepare to lead, whether it is one session or the entire series, here are a few thoughts to keep in mind. We encourage you to read these and review them with each new discussion leader before he or she leads.

1.   *Remember that you are not alone.*

God knows everything about you, and He knew that you would be asked to lead your group. Remember that it is common for all good leaders to feel that they are not ready to lead. Moses, Solomon, Jeremiah, and Timothy were all reluctant to lead. God promises, *"Never will I leave you; never will I forsake you"* (Hebrews 13:5). Whether you are leading for one evening, for several weeks, or for a lifetime, you will be blessed as you serve.

2.   *Don't try to do it alone.*

Pray right now for God to help you build a healthy leadership team. If you can enlist a co-leader to help you lead the group, you will find your experience to be much richer. This is your chance to involve as many people as you can in building a healthy group. All you have to do is call and ask people to help. You'll probably be surprised at the response.

3.   *Just be yourself.*

If you won't be you, who will? God wants you to use your unique gifts and temperament. Don't try to do things exactly like another leader; do them in a way that fits you! Just admit it when you don't have an answer, and apologize when you make a mistake. Your group will love you for it, and you'll sleep better at night!

4.   *Prepare for your meeting ahead of time.*

Review the session and the leader's notes, and write down your responses to each question. Pay special attention to exercises that ask group members to do something other than engage in discussion. These exercises will help your group live what the Bible teaches, not just talk about it. Be sure you understand how an exercise works, and bring any necessary supplies (such as paper and pens) to your meeting. If the exercise employs one of the items in the appendix, be sure to look over that item so you'll know how it works. Finally, review "Outline for Each Session" so you'll remember the purpose of each section in the study.

5.   *Pray for your group members by name.*

Before you begin your session, go around the room in your mind and pray for each member by name. You may want to review the prayer list at least once a week. Ask God to use your time together to touch the heart of every person uniquely. Expect God to lead you to whomever He wants you to encourage or challenge in a special way. If you listen, God will surely lead!

6.   *When you ask a question, be patient.*

Someone will eventually respond. Sometimes people need a moment or two of silence to think about the question. Keep in mind, if silence doesn't bother you, it won't bother anyone else. After someone responds, affirm the response with a simple "thanks" or "good job." Then ask, "How about somebody else?" or "Would someone who hasn't shared like to add anything?" Be sensitive to new people or reluctant members who aren't ready to say, pray, or do anything. If you give them a safe setting, they will blossom over time.

7.   *Provide transitions between questions.*

When guiding the discussion, always read aloud the transitional paragraphs and the questions. Ask the group if anyone would like to read the paragraph or Bible passage. Don't call on anyone, but ask for a volunteer, and then be patient until someone begins. Be sure to thank the person who reads aloud.

8.   *Break up into smaller groups each week or they won't stay.*

If your group has more than seven people, we strongly encourage you to have the group gather sometimes in discussion circles of three or four people. With a greater opportunity to talk in a small circle, people will connect more with the study, apply more quickly what they're learning, and ultimately get more out of it. A small circle also encourages a quiet person to participate and tends to minimize the effects of a more vocal or dominant member. It can also help people feel more loved in your group. When you gather again at the end of the section, you can have one person summarize the highlights from each circle. Small circles are also helpful during prayer time. People who are unaccustomed to praying aloud will feel more comfortable trying it with just two or three others. Also, prayer requests won't take as much time, so circles will have more time to actually pray. When you gather back with the whole group, you can have one person from each circle briefly update everyone on the prayer requests. People are more willing to pray in small circles if they know that the whole group will hear all the prayer requests.

9.   *Rotate facilitators weekly.*

At the end of each meeting, ask the group who should lead the following week. Let the group help select your weekly facilitator. You may be perfectly capable of leading each time, but you will help others grow in their faith and gifts if you give them opportunities to lead. You can use the Small Group Calendar to fill in the names of all meeting leaders at once if you prefer.

10.   *One final challenge (for new or first-time leaders):*

Before your first opportunity to lead, look up each of the five passages listed below. Read each one as a devotional exercise to help yourself develop a shepherd's heart. Trust us on this one. If you do this, you will be more than ready for your first meeting.

- Matthew 9:36

- 1 Peter 5:2-4

- Psalm 23

- Ezekiel 34:11-16

- 1 Thessalonians 2:7-8, 11-12

Notes

About Troy Brewer

Troy Brewer is a tireless student of God's Word and sold-out believer in all things prophetic. Pastor at OpenDoor Church in Burleson, Texas, Troy's radio and television programs are broadcast worldwide. He is a global missionary known for his radical love for Jesus, unique teaching style, and his passion for serving people. Troy rescues girls and boys from sex trafficking worldwide through his ministry, Troy Brewer Ministries.

OTHER BOOKS BY TROY A. BREWER

Numbers That Preach

Living Life /Forward

Good Overcomes Evil

Looking Up

Soul Invasion

Daily Transformation Devotional

Miracles with a Message

Best of the Brewer

BE THE BAD MOTOR SCOOTER
YOU WERE MEANT TO BE!

Partner with Troy to free slaves worldwide and get access to Troy's revelational teachings as your reward!

Your monthly sponsorship not only rescues slaves from the horrors of sex trafficking and gives them the food, shelter, medical care, education, and job skills they need to live a transformed life in King Jesus, your gift also gives you 24/7 access to Troy's on-demand teaching service.

At TroyBrewer.TV, you can access life-changing conferences, sermon series, and prophetic revelations on any device from anywhere in the world.

When you partner with Troy to bring liberty to the captives, you'll be transformed and so will they.

Sign up at TroyBrewer.com, TroyBrewer.TV or call 877.413.0888.

Made in the USA
Monee, IL
28 January 2021